The Trouble with Training

A Book by Bob Chapman
Copyright 2018

A Companion to
The Training Professional's Handbook © 2013

Introduction

The trouble with training is NOT that everyone is a trainer at heart. No, contrary to what training professionals might have you think, people have a unique ability to recognize what good training looks like, even if they don't have the grasp of the concepts and methodology.

I strongly believe that people understand good training, and even though they may not be able or equipped to provide that level of learning, they are surely capable of critiquing and providing quantitative feedback to the contrary when it doesn't exist.

The trouble with training is more grounded in the precepts of personal malaise, or an organization's unwillingness to dedicate time, effort, or money to its success.

The Training function owns this—an organization's inability to see the value in learning and performance is usually based on the lack of value it has seen in the past, or the lack of value a Training Department has produced.

Training involves marketing as much as it does enhancing skills and knowledge, and this arena leaves most L&P (Learning & Performance) departments high and dry. A leader's inability to sell and promote their products to the masses is of great dismay, as many talented training specialists are left high, dry, and unnoticed by their companies.

Out of Touch with Reality

There's nothing worse than a training function that's lost its grip on reality. And by reality, I am referring to the business imperatives that make a company run. Training staffs that think they have the pre-destined plan to solve all the organizational woes has no concept of the true nature of business—that it is dynamic and ever-evolving. Having a plan is a good thing, but being inflexible in that plan make L&P seem out of touch.

Continuously network and meet with stake holders to ensure their needs and desires haven't changed over time, and you'll discover that their needs have changed. The vision may remain steadfast, but the key strategies and prioritized initiatives have indeed.

A Lack of Vision

To me there is nothing more detrimental to an organization than a lack of Vision. Without it, there's just a bunch of well-intended people who come to work each day, do what they think is best, then go home at the day's end. They're not unified, or able to prioritize based on Vision Priorities…they're just talented, misguided workers. Have a vision, and work for a company that has a clearly articulated vision.

My current company is one such beast. It is frustrating to no end. I remember since day one, asking, "What's our Vision?" The answer was, "Own Safety", and things along those lines. Well, if we were a safety company that would make sense. Safety should be a part of every company's goal…but it's not the Vision. We have no clear path forward, no ambition or goal…just to be safe while we're doing whatever it is we're supposed to be doing. No end game--no future state.

It causes me great distraught daily, I assure you. I will not be long at this company, believe me.

Vision is the cornerstone of success and a rallying cry for all to understand and acknowledge.

Great companies have great visions, and more specifically, the visions are easy for all to grasp and understand. It's not the complexity of the vision that makes it grand, it's the relevance to each employee. Conversely, poor companies have ambiguous visions, or assume that the nature of the business dictates the vision, such as an oil refinery's vision simply being, "make gasoline—safely, of course."

It could be more appropriate that the vision clearly define the "why" like "Fueling the World with the Energy of Today" or something close. Why companies do what they do, is more important than what they do. Training has to be aligned with the why as much as the how and what.

Training Departments also fail when they lack a vision as well, regardless of the company's short-sightedness to produce one. Every department should be aligned around a common cause, and their specific key strategies will differ, but the end result should be unanimous.

Some have told me that they tend to find a disconnect in vision based on the overarching business function they report to. I have been part of Human Resources, Operations, and even Engineering and Reliability. True, the "umbrella" of who Training reports to can change the overall agenda—and alter the prioritization of needs throughout any given year or business plan, but the credo has to remain true.

The vision I hold true to most is one that to me has been interchangeable over decades…it's not an epiphany or a call to action, so to speak, but it resonates with me, and I adjust it slightly depending on the organization I'm working with at the time.

"Providing consistent, innovative and high value learning solutions across all business units to drive results and enhance our competitive advantage. Training must be relevant, real world, and its outcomes measurable. Providing the right training to the right people at the right time for the right reasons is imperative."

Translated—be the Rock Stars of Learning!

I cannot stress the importance and criticality of having a Vision!

A Disconnect between Objectives and Bloom's Taxonomy

Training gets a bad rap, and understandably so, in the relationship between learning objectives and course content, leading to many long term shortcomings. Not that course content is awful; it's just that objective writing missed the mark.

First, let's look at some components of Bloom's Taxonomy, and weave it into the development of better course objectives.

Appealing to basic human desires is crucial to effective transfer of concepts. (Bloom's Taxonomy)

In 1956, Benjamin Bloom headed a group of educational psychologists who developed a classification of levels of intellectual behavior important in learning.

Learning is meant to affect individuals in a variety of

ways. Well developed, thoughtful curriculum, delivered appropriately by an accomplished training professional, should strike at the human condition in 3 ways.

These 3 ways, or **Learning Domains** are:

>**Cognitive** (the actual knowledge provided)
>
>**Affective** (the emotional result of training)
>
>**Psychomotor** (the physical, or behavioral changes associated with training)

Bloom then determined that within the Cognitive Domain, there is a logical progression that training is meant to provoke on an ascending scale. These are:

>**Knowledge** – Ability to recall information or data
>
>**Comprehension** - Understand the meaning, translation, and interpretation of instructions and problems. State a problem in one's own words.
>
>**Application** - Use a concept in a new situation or unprompted use of an abstraction. Applies what was learned in the classroom into novel situations in the work place.

Analysis - Separates material or concepts into component parts so that its organizational structure may be understood. Distinguishes between facts and inferences.

Synthesis - Builds a structure or pattern from diverse elements. Put parts together to form a whole, with emphasis on creating a new meaning or structure.

Evaluation - Make judgments about the value of ideas or materials

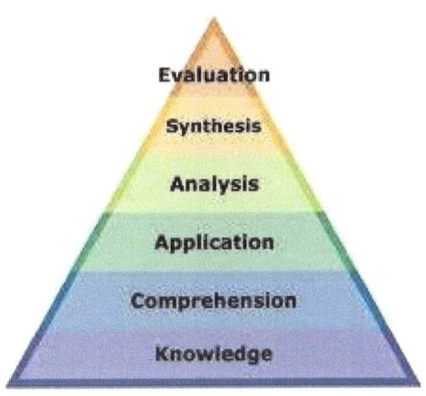

The pyramid is inverted to better represent the hierarchy of ascension.

Bloom's Revised Taxonomy

Lorin Anderson, a former student of Bloom, revisited the cognitive domain in the learning taxonomy in the mid-nineties and made some changes, with perhaps the two most prominent ones being, 1) changing the names in the six categories from noun to verb forms, and 2) slightly rearranging them.

This new taxonomy reflects a more active form of thinking and is perhaps more accurate:

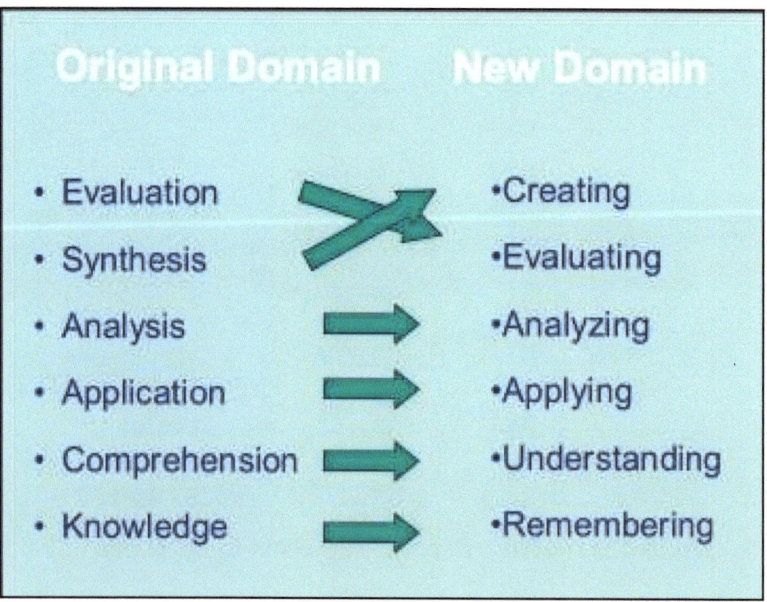

The goal for a training professional is to achieve Synthesis, or Creating, not only in their personal occupations, but to also guide individuals to that pinnacle as well. As I had been told many times over the years, the result of training is that we develop people to be able to take the information we have shared so that they then go forth and continue that training with others. For anyone to successfully accomplish this, we need to help them through the taxonomy.

While we as facilitators cannot control who our learners are, or how they learn, we can ensure that our delivery methods are equitable and delivered in a manner that allows all learners the best opportunities possible.

The problems occur when we develop our course or topic objectives before building actual content.

How many times have you attended a class and the basic "Objectives" slide read something like this:

Upon successful completion of this course of study the participant will be able to:
State the parts of a bicycle
Understand the maintenance requirements for a bicycle
Demonstrate the ability to safely operate a bicycle

Seems perfectly fine, right? Well, let's examine them closer and bounce these objectives off of Bloom's Taxonomy and see how effective the training will be.

Think in terms of the hierarchy of knowledge, and what we're trying to achieve. We'd like an employee who is capable of being self-directed, and can in turn teach others all there is to know about cycling and the processes involved.

Creating

Evaluating

Analyzing

Applying

Understanding

Remembering

So with our first objective, "State the parts of a bicycle", which component are we addressing?

If you answered "**Remembering**" then you're correct!

Our second objective is relatively clear cut. "Understand the maintenance requirements for a bicycle."

Yes, it focuses on "**Understanding**."

So that brings us to our third objective, "Demonstrate the ability to safely operate a bicycle."

You already know exactly where I'm going with this, don't you?

Creating

Evaluating

Analyzing

Applying

Understanding

Remembering

Most would say that a demonstration revealed the ability to effectively "**Apply**" learning.

Many would consider this an effective training session, focusing on the first three levels of the Taxonomy, but we as training professionals want more…we want our organizations to succeed long-term, and the problem is, with this Bicycle Class, and the myriad of others we conduct or design during the span of a career, we've done nothing to perpetuate a climate of self-learning!

Creating

Evaluating

Analyzing

Applying   **Demonstrate the ability to safely operate a bicycle**
Understanding   **Understand the maintenance requirements for a bicycle**
Remembering   **State the parts of a bicycle**

I am one to believe that any session shouldn't incorporate too many objectives. My personal philosophy has been 3-5 objectives maximum. But our focus has to improve on what those objectives are…precisely and accurately. We've got to be able to nail down objectives that are concise and reflective of the outcome we truly want. Our job is to influence the outcome through a deep understanding of the design and development of materials and methods.

So, how could we revise the objectives, or scrap them altogether, so our design efforts are creating the most value for the participant, and the organization?

Creating

Evaluating

Analyzing

Applying

Understanding

Remembering

Again, for simplicity's sake, let's stick with just three objectives.

Upon successful completion of this topic, the participant will be able to:

1) Recognize and determine the appropriate maintenance requirements for bicycles in use

2) Evaluate the safe operation and components necessary for riders to perform

3) Develop and create a comprehensive Bicycle Maintenance and Safety Program for employees to use at the site

Creating	**Develop and create a comprehensive Bicycle Maintenance and Safety Program for employees to use at the site**
Evaluating	**Evaluate the safe operation and components necessary for riders to perform**
Analyzing	**Recognize and determine the appropriate maintenance requirements for bicycles in use**
Applying	
Understanding	
Remembering	

By doing this, we have shifted the level of learning to a more self-sustaining program, and development based on these objectives will substantially increase participation and involvement.

This is not to say that Remembering, Understanding, and Applying aren't important—they certainly are. They work best in a basic, introductory level course of study, and are a valuable part of any learning environment. I just want you to think of all the verbs we tend to throw around so freely when we're determining training needs, like the ones listed below:

State   Understand   Recognize   Demonstrate

Conduct   Perform   Repeat   Identify

When your constituents start tossing around verbs like these, they should instantly send up "red flags" to you, and signal your time to intervene to discover what outcomes your customers really want. A deeper insight into objectives can help improve credibility and sustainability of any learning event.

Content and Training's Viability with the 70/20/10 Concept

First off, I am not advocating the 70-20-10 concept…I know there have been enough people trying to debunk its credibility for some time. To me, yes, the numbers are too rounded, but in theory it represents the struggle we all face in the L&P arena—we're just NOT significant enough! Sad but true. Like it or not. To use a phrase my co-workers abhor—"It is what it is."

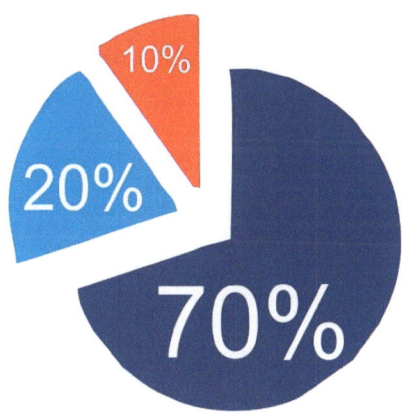

So just what is this concept of 70-20-10? It is a learning and development model of 70% challenging assignments, 20% developmental relationships and 10% coursework and training. Morgan McCall and his colleagues working at the Center for Creative Leadership (CCL) are usually credited with originating the 70:20:10 ratio. Two of McCall's colleagues, Michael M. Lombardo and Robert W. Eichinger, published data from one CCL study in their 1996 book *The Career Architect Development Planner*.

Based on a survey asking nearly 200 executives to self-report how they believed they learned, McCall, Lombardo and Eichinger's surmised that: "Lessons learned by successful and effective managers are roughly:

70% from challenging assignments

20% from developmental relationships

10% from coursework and training

Lombardo and Eichinger expressed their rationale behind the 70:20:10 model this way in *The Career Architect Development Planner*:

"Development generally begins with a realization of current or future need and the motivation to do something about it. This might come from feedback, a mistake, watching other people's reactions, failing or not being up to a task – in other words, from experience. The odds are that development will be about 70% from on-the-job experiences - working on tasks and problems; about 20% from feedback and working around good and bad examples of the need; and 10% from courses and reading."

In recent years, many academics have been coming out against the purported effectiveness of the 70-20-10 hypothesis. Criticisms include:

A lack of empirical supporting data

The use of perfectly even numbers

The nature of the survey (i.e. Asking already successful managers to reflect on their experiences.)

It is often suggested that the model does not reflect the changes in the market instigated by online technologies. For example, it does not reflect the recent focus on informal learning.

While the model may serve to inspire some to consider non-formal learning as a part of their learning programs, it's important to remember that 70:20:10 was never intended to be a prescriptive model. Learning professionals are encouraged to remember that 70:20:10 "is neither a scientific fact nor a recipe for how best to develop people."

It is, however, a basis for argument to the validity of a Training Department.

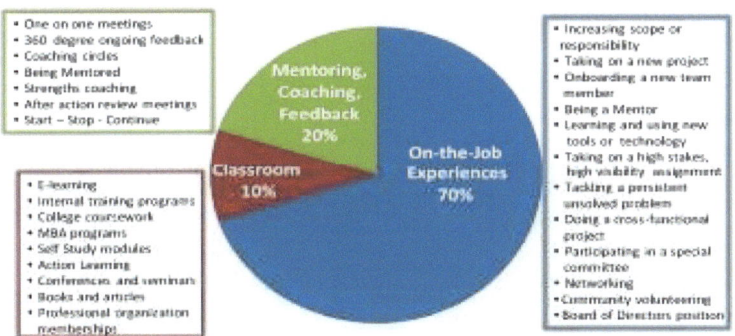

Allocating more time to experiential, applied learning yields better development and business outcomes.

I believe this is a decent structure for validating successes in training—or at least to help justify why we still need to exist!

Although the numbers may vary some, formalized training programs play a small role in an individual's overall success. Therefore, the savvy training professional must seek out new ways to become involved.

To help illustrate my point, I created this seemingly harmless graphic:

The best in class training systems borrow a few percentage points from the "20% Feedback & Coaching" portion, provided we work to help develop leaders and supervisory skills. So it is possible that the numbers tilt a bit, perhaps 68/18/14…or something similar, but even then, formal training is far from the lion's share of personal and professional development. Its critical then, that we involve ourselves in as many "post-training" endeavors as we can, to include refresher training down the road. A hands-on approach works best for an employee life cycle.

To help illustrate my point behind this whole concept:

10% of our driving proficiency came from studying the training aids and Rules of the Road. The requisites were turning 16 and having a permit and a car. We then worked on becoming (Qualified).

20% was transferred from your father or mother through On-the-Road/Behind the Wheel coaching. After hours of driving and study we took the Written and Practical Skills Tests and became (Certified).

70%...BUT... Not until we have driven in snow, rain, fog, sand, high speeds and low, sunshine and darkness, on back roads and congested highways, fixed flats, towed and been towed, for years…do we have any iota of (Proficiency).

To me, the same holds true of the entire 70/20/10 concept. An individual requires certain regulatory, or foundational fundamental training, then gains experience through the time spent with qualified workers, learning and receiving coaching and feedback. But not until they have experienced upset conditions, things outside normal operating parameters, and dealing with crisis and emergencies are they truly gaining proficiency.

As training professionals, we have to recognize this to be true, and work to immerse ourselves in a "cradle to grave" training mentality.

Failing to Anticipate the Customer's Needs

Arrogant or seasoned trainers have this baggage known as the "curse of knowledge", a mental model that holds to the premise that, if I know something, I expect others to know it as intimately and as well as I do. Illustrated, an experiment on the curse of knowledge went like this: a group of people were given a list of songs to tap out on a table…no other melodies—just tapping the rhythm with their fingers. A group of listeners were expected to guess the songs accurately. Although the tappers could internally hear the song with perfect clarity, the listeners were unable to determine any of the songs—it merely sounded like a series of endless finger taps to them. Thus, a training professional might hear the needs of a customer in their minds with great precision, but fails to articulate or explain in the detail needed to help the customer understand the process.

To this end, customers grow increasingly disappointed with the output and involvement from trainers or curriculum designers.

We've got to prepare for "creative destruction," and anticipate the customer's needs, listen to them carefully, and then partner with them to provide the best solutions.

Enthusiasm and Innovation Issues

Let's face it; we've all been in training sessions. Each of us has a lifetime of experience with the good, the bad, and the ugly of training. We've either been the victim or the blade-wielder or such events. And none of us, not a single one, wants to be bludgeoned with the mundane and humdrum. We want excitement, enthusiasm, and a level of concern and professionalism unsurpassed. We not only want these things—we need them! Our brains are wired to be entertained and enlightened. Boring training doesn't help us understand, it doesn't help us engage, and it doesn't stick.

Trainers who take the time to hone their craft and find ways to motivate and inspire are what we lack—and I'm not referring to motivational speakers…I hate that term, "motivational speakers." To me it invokes thoughts of a one-sided monologue…sit back and listen to me…I'm an expert…I'm up here and you're down there…let me spew out knowledge in an interesting way, collect my paycheck, then I'm moving on to the next Ted Talk or appearance.

Motivational speakers have little investment in the continued cycle of learning. They are a circus act, a one-trick pony who steals profits from every company they speak for.

I've seen companies fall victim to NASCAR speakers, Blind Hunters, Accident Victims, Politicians, and of course, those who simply tout themselves as "motivational speakers" whose repertoire is as vast and definable as money will allow.

I always resist such speakers when asked about their value…always opting to cultivate either an in-house expert, or someone locally in a similar, or sister industry. If it's shock and awe you're after, then go ahead and hire one. If it's continued education and development, find another mechanism. They're out there, trust me.

Train-the-Trainer Workshops are fine for helping non-professional employees garner the necessary tools to become better at presenting, but even most Train-the-Trainer Workshops are focused on a specific genre, or type of training. I go for the more holistic approach to training trainers...something that provides the why, how, and what. TO me these are core principles.

Helping people add enthusiasm to their capability is often impossible. It's easier to identify stellar characters and then teach them how to teach, than it is to identify teachers and teach them how to interact and excite others. Just my personal opinion, but over time—like 30 plus years—I've not been surprised by the results.

Organizations should always seek out those individuals that have a list of pre-disposed character traits that enhance training. They may be well-regarded, highly charismatic, truly concerned, or deeply driven to help others. They're there—every organization has their rock star trainers…we just have to identify who they are and provide some fundamental tools for them.

CEOs may always get the most laughs from their jokes, but spectacular trainers glean the most value.

Find your innovators. Find those who aren't afraid to challenge the status quo, for therein lies success. Too often "challengers" aren't viewed as champions, they're viewed as trouble. Contrary to HR's beliefs, they add excitement and an innovative curve to training, and overall development.

Lagging Technology

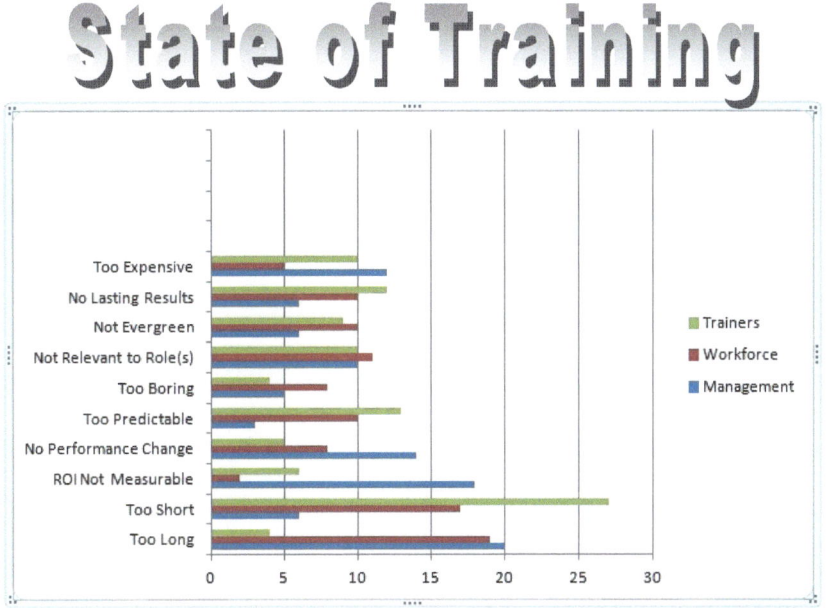

This chart was derived by surveying 1,000 individuals in 3 categories: Management, Workforce, and Trainers. It revealed the disparity between how certain tiers of an organization tend to view training overall. The surveys were sent to similar industries, for more accurate results, and these were the Top 10

Recurring Themes. Another interesting finding was, although not reflected on the chart, questions dealing with the different age groups at an organization, Baby Boomer, Gen X, Millennial, Gen Y, and their perspectives on technology used to stimulate and provoke thought. Many thought that methods used were antiquated and outdated, and there should be more use of social media and Smart Technology to enhance and improve learning.

Many expect the L&P function to provide these advancements, or to at least be ambassadors for change, and keeping an altruistic point of view on the overall state of learning methodologies. I agree. If not us, who?

Surveying tools, interactive apps, presentations, all can be found at the click of a keypad. Many companies pay good money to outfit their employees with smart phones, yet shy away from having them use them to our advantage. How many times have you been in a classroom setting and one of the first requests of Class Norms from the facilitator is "Please put your cell phones on vibrate, or turn them off, please." To me, nothing could be more contrary to what we want to achieve! I want people to use their phones, conduct research with them, perhaps even use some gamification tools to draw in their audience. So please, if you're that "vibrate your cell phone" type of instructor, seriously consider changing your MO! Embrace technology—be on the cusp of the new and innovative!

Not Identifying and Developing Trainers

As I'd mentioned earlier, there is a plethora of decent trainers at any company. They may not be, however, the first candidate a supervisor pulls for you when you request someone to serve in the role. Chances are, from a supervisory perspective, the leader is searching for someone senior, with vast knowledge of the technical aspects of a job or function, and doesn't look at those folks with less experience in the role, but more experience as am extroverted presenter. It's important that the training team get involved, be observant, and solicit candidates that best fir the situation.

Over the course of my career I've helped thousands of people receive certifications, attend self-improvement classes, achieve journeyman status, yet often fail to continuously improve myself. This is perhaps true of most trainers—their sole focus is on their customers, rarely on themselves.

Maintaining currency in the marketplace is an operational imperative. Understanding the newest technologies, resources, and delivery methods helps build a level of excellence within your organization.

Each member of a training team, be they instructional designers, training specialists, administrative assistants, managers, organizational development consultants, should have or develop a personal development plan. This should outline goals and certifications or courses desired. Align them with the organization's priorities and you'll have a decent plan to work with.

Take the time to develop and help your teams remain on the cutting edge of things that are new, and qualifications that set your team apart from others in industry.

Individual Development Plan

Refer to the User Guide section on page 2 for form instructions.

Employee Name:		Date:	
Department:		Position/Title:	

Goals for success in your current role:	

Short-term development goal(s):	

Development Objective	Development Activities *(Training, projects, books etc.)*	Proposed Comp Date	Start Date	Date Completed

Long-term development goal(s):	Work toward developing the skills necessary to lead a Learning Organization.

Development Objective	Development Activities *(Training, projects, books etc.)*	Proposed Comp Date	Start Date	Date Completed

Notes:

Employee signature _____ Supervisor signature _____

This is merely a sample of an Individual Development Plan. Work in concert with your supervisor to make sure you lay out a road map toward success.

Comparative versus Competitive Advantage

When we consider the alternatives that departments or companies have to select from for their training needs, specifically external vendors, we should involve ourselves in their decisions to the extent we are able and allowed to. There's nothing wrong with hiring external training vendors, in fact, many times we just don't have the capability or can't issue certain state of federal certifications that may be required, so it's necessary to develop ongoing relationships with vendors as a whole.

When it comes to measuring our own effectiveness, internally, we need to do a better job at recognizing the comparative advantages of our training staff, as well as the competitive advantages they bring as a team.

If the concept of comparative and competitive advantage is new to you, allow me to explain a bit more.

A person's comparative advantage is that at which she creates more value than she could given her other options. One's comparative advantage can change with one's skills, the skills of other team members, or the needs of the team. An organization's success depends in part on its ability to motivate and empower people to find and exercise their comparative advantages.

Competitive advantage, on the other hand, is the collective talents and capabilities of the department, organization, or business.

Recognizing individual skills is a crucial element of leadership, and then leveraging those skills to gain the most value. In training, determining the skills is equally important. Cross-functional capabilities lead to more cohesion, and a trainer who is also adept at creating videos, or with curriculum design builds on the team's overall abilities. An LMS guru who is also a competent presenter goes a long way to success. Each of us have to determine comparative advantages, and then work to increase the advantages we possess. The more we improve comparative advantage, the more we inherently increase competitive advantage, or edge, over our competitors.

Training can be Very Expensive
Where's the ROI?

If you have a comprehensive answer for this, you've just won the jackpot. This question is posed and pondered at all levels of any company. Financial strategies are risked around it, and the value of training is dependent upon how well we can provide data.

There have been tangible metrics I've used in the past, but still it seems subjective in nature. To the extent one can truly determine training effectiveness is arbitrary at best.

- Participant Satisfaction Surveys (Course Critiques)
- Supervisory Positions Open < 30 days
- Site Leadership effectiveness assessment (annually)
- Observed Behaviors in the Workplace
- # of Delinquent Performance Reviews > 30 days
- Unplanned Attrition Reduction below 10%
- Reduction in B/C Events by 10% each monitoring period
- Reduction in Safety Incidents and Environmental Incidents

- Cost per attendee versus increase in output

Again, the variables depend on the type of business, as well as whether you're trying to measure sales goals...which is easier to conduct based on actual hard data in sales reports, or whether you're trying to measure the success of leadership development programs, which require a combination of different metrics, some which still might not be affected totally by training.

Any conversations with your constituents will help maintain direct dialogue and prevents any pre-conceived notions of measurements of return on investments.

From a regulatory perspective, having properly qualified and certified technicians prevents fines or penalties from being incurred, so those statistics should be readily available, ie. The cost of one employee not being qualified in the eyes of OSHA or

EPA standards can be calculated and documented. There can be an exact dollar amount affixed to those. Just as there have always been exact dollar amounts affixed to a "First Aid" injury at a manufacturing plant. Any Safety Department should have that figure readily available.

Maintenance is another area where skills can easily be broken down into dollars. The cost of a mechanic having to do "re-work" to repair the same piece of equipment is sunk cost and opportunity cost squandered. The amount of labor hours, equipment replacement or repair costs, along with lost production will equate to a specific dollar amount as well.

Being aware of market alternatives, the business' financials, and developing conversation with stakeholders, and always having a strategy trumps the usual "shrug of the shoulders" one get when asking what the cost of training will be.

Another area to monitor is the high cost of external training sources. Some of these are for actual training presentations, others are for the maintenance of LMS systems, or libraries of computer based training (CBT) modules. There is a plethora of services vendors are willing to provide, from procedure writing to training manual development and maintenance—all of which come with a hefty price tag. Negotiate, and shop around. Don't become comfortable or reliant on any single source—every business has a competitor.

In the petrochemical world, it's nothing to drop $60k on a 200 course CBT library, annually! Or $15k for a tri-annual crane certification course for 5 employees. Monitor spending, and if it's coming from another department's budget, help them manage costs by getting involved.

Another area to check periodically is external training at vendor locations, not "in-house." I've discovered on more than one occasion, different departments wanted to send their folks to "The Seven Habits of Highly Effective People" and the workshop was being held in Houston at the time.

4 different departments sent 2 people each—separate of each other—to the workshop. Had I known ahead of time I could have negotiated group rates, consolidated transportation, or even had an in-house class held which would have saved thousands. Look around, it's happening more often than you think. When training isn't viewed as culpable, departments will strike out on their own to seize any opportunity they can. This normally results in exorbitant fees and a non-customized approach.

Not Considering Motivation Theory in Adults

Facilitators don't have to be the most eloquent speakers or the most knowledgeable. They don't have to be the foremost authority on subject matter nor do they have to possess the greatest amount of corporate knowledge. They must, however, be able to relate their groups' experiences to the topic, and they must be regarded as someone who is genuine, authentic, and concerned.

The most difficult task in adult learning is motivating participants to learn and exchange their ideas. This matter requires constant attention. The facilitator who is capable of motivating and captivating their audience is also capable of passing on a positive educational experience to all.

In this segment, we will discuss various aspects of motivation and how it drives group dynamics and individual learning, and how the facilitator is the catalyst.

Adults share some intrinsic characteristics relative to learning. They are:

Interest- Adults are looking for something interesting to occupy their time. They are looking to be entertained, while also having a product of value delivered to them. Keep your presentations interesting and keep your participants involved. So remember:

- Adults want something interesting
- Adults want it fun and dynamic
- Adults want a positive experience
- Adults want something relevant and "real world"
- Adults want commonality with their instructor

Needs- Adults have needs that must be met. Breaks are important, the average adult needs to unwind every 50-60 minutes. That doesn't mean that breaks need to be 10 or 15 minutes. Often just a short reprieve is all that's required. Adults also need to know that their participation is valued, so thank them when they do. Depending on your audience, there may also be business that must be tended to. If there is something emergent, let them know they can slip out and take care of that business in the hallway or elsewhere. Adults also need the restroom more often than their younger counterparts, so again, refer to giving breaks often. So remember:

- Learners have basic needs to be met
- Learners have a desire to be heard
- Learners should be allowed input into learning
- Learners want to be well-regarded by peers
- Learners want to learn

Adult Level- Adults also have the ability to evaluate, so don't think for a moment that they're not evaluating you constantly. Be fair, treat each member with respect, and do right by your class. Adults, although they enjoy humor, don't like being treated like children. Keep the information at an adult level, don't patronize or belittle them. So remember:

- Adults want to be treated as adults
- Adults need breaks
- Adults need positive interaction with each other
- Adults have the ability to evaluate!
- Adults can be very candid
- Adults learn in portions
- Adults expect "fair play"

Values- This kind of goes hand in hand with doing things on an adult level. Adults have deeply ingrained value systems, so be cautious not to tread on them. You give what you get, is often a good policy to abide by. So remember:

- Learners have personal values
- Learners have company values
- Learners have ethical standards
- Learners must comply with company policies

Incentives- Everyone wants some type of incentive, whether that's getting finished a bit early because participation was so good, or various forms of recognition to class members when they respond properly. Always seek to discover new ways to incentivize your training. So remember:

- Adults thrive when there are rewards
- Adults will participate more when inspired to do so
- Adults may be reluctant to be in class at first
- Adults like to be told they did something well

Achievement- As always, adults want to know what the end game is—what's in it for them. There has got to be a reason you've brought them together today, so make that clear when discussing objectives, expectations, and going forward. So remember:

- Learners like to know the "end game"
- Learners want management to allow them to use their skills or learning
- Learners want to know what's in it for them
- Learners want to know management appreciates their successes
- Learners want to make sure the training will actually help them

We as professionals in learning and development must always be aware of our audience, and go the extra mile to insure we appease the basic needs that garner their devotion to our training efforts.

Not Having a Strong Marketing Campaign

Another area where everyone could use help is with a strategic marketing, or advertising campaign. Often, we assume that people will search the LMS to find new topics and courses to attend, that they will be on a never ending quest for development, but this just isn't the case. Business gets in the way of education, and we need to remain relevant, and in the forefront, so a sound marketing plan is essential.

Whether you use Newsletters, E-Newsletters, E-Mail Promotions, training calendars or company event calendars, bulletin boards, company directories, or have a vocal salesperson at your avail to discuss the merits of upcoming training and the need for continuous needs analysis, there are plenty of venues at your disposal. It's really a matter of recognizing them, developing them if they don't exist, and seizing the opportunity to promote your team.

I've seen some departments send out monthly Employee Bios so that everyone could become familiar with some of the qualifications, or personal side of each other. It helps to find that level of commonality that was discussed in the Motivation Theory section previously.

I have used monthly newsletters, both electronic and paper copies—I always distribute the paper copies to break rooms, conference rooms, and any other places large groups assemble, because I am aware that often leadership "filters" their communications, and not everyone has immediate access to a computer in the conduct of their daily jobs, so to me it's always been important that hard copies be handed out so everyone gains exposure and can see the opportunities available to them.

Your greatest allies should be your executive management teams, but even the newest employee needs to understand what it is, what you can do, and how there is benefit to them personally for learning and development.

I often make sure that courses are open to the public, not exclusively for those who might require the training, for example, opening a Refining Economics course to anyone interested (provided their supervisor is onboard with it), and not just folks in Procurement, or Optimization. Naturally, if size or seats are limited, or on a "per head" basis, then I hold seats so that the right people who need the training get it.

Your campaign doesn't have to be fancy or flashy—although it helps—the important thing is that you need to advertise your value!

Every role requires a degree of salesmanship, and in today's business climate this seems truer than ever.

In Conclusion

Over time there will be more "companion" books to this subject, as there is not a singular answer or cure-all to the issues surrounding effective, high quality training endeavors. It is the culmination of talented individuals aligned to a common cause, the professional development of employees delivered in an enthusiastic, memorable way that aids in a self-sustaining learning culture.

Challenge your people to excel, challenge yourself to improve and avoid the pitfalls that befall even world class organizations.

Training is one of those departments where everyone is a critic, and everyone has a vision of what "ideal" should look like. Seek out feedback, take a realistic look at your current state, then strategize to achieve that "best in class" persona for your team.

I'm sure there are other critical areas I have overlooked, or forgotten to mention. I welcome your feedback, thoughts, and concerns. When all is said and done, we're all in this business together, and continuous process improvement is the nature of the beast.

On the bright side, this book didn't end up being hundreds of pages in length, so there is hope for the future of training! It's not all doom and gloom, and there are fabulous programs being implemented all across the globe. Competent organizations recognize deep in their hearts the overall value and necessity for a strong, lasting training structure, and will fund their existence. We've got to be ahead of the game, identifying new opportunities and methods, building our teams internally and identifying and hiring candidates who can help perpetuate us into the future. In twenty years the face of learning and performance will change dramatically—I can't even fathom what shape it will evolve into—but employees will still need the support and development provided by concerned, compassionate training teams. As I've been told repeatedly, "If you're not part of the solution, then you're part of the problem."

Be the solution.

Let's make a change.

Other Companion Books by Bob Chapman

The Training Professional's Handbook

Non-Fiction/Business "How To" Guide; Published 2013

Guide to the development and creation of a Learning and Performance platform.

Tubes of Empty Lip Gloss; Smashing Through the Wall of Our Own Design--A Practical Guide to Overcoming the Phenomenon of "Writer's Block" Through a Series of Exercises and Short Prose

Non-Fiction/Business/Writing "How To" Guide; Published 2018

Inspirational and practical guide to overcoming "writer's block."

www.ingramcontent.com/pod-product-compliance
Lightning Source LLC
Chambersburg PA
CBHW040238220526
45473CB00001B/288